BEST OF GORDON LIGHTFOOT

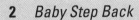

Cover photo courtesy of Warner Bros. Records/Photofest

ISBN 978-1-4950-0685-2

HAL•LEONARD®
CORPORATION

7777 W. BLUEMOUND RD. P.O. BOX 13819 MILWAUKEE, WI 53213

In Australia Contact:
Hal Leonard Australia Pty. Ltd.
4 Lentara Court
Cheltenham, Victoria, 3192 Australia
Email: ausadmin@halleonard.com.au

Visit Hal Leonard Online at
www.halleonard.com

BABY STEP BACK

Words and Music by
GORDON LIGHTFOOT

Moderately

Now, it

looks to __ me __ like the same __ old place. __ In the sky, it looks like __ rain. __

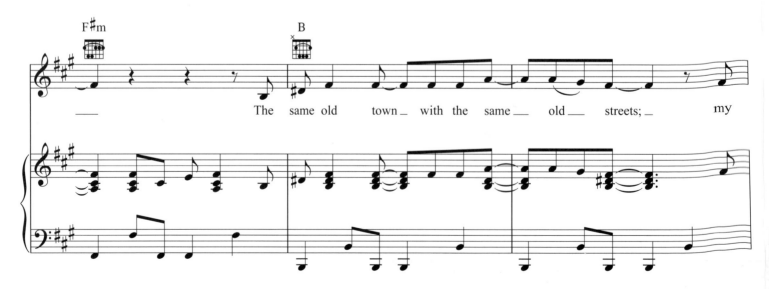

__ The same old town __ with the same __ old __ streets; __ my

3

BEAUTIFUL

Words and Music by
GORDON LIGHTFOOT

Moderately

At times   I   just don't   know __
Laugh - ing eyes   and smil - ing   face; __
And when   you hold me   tight, __

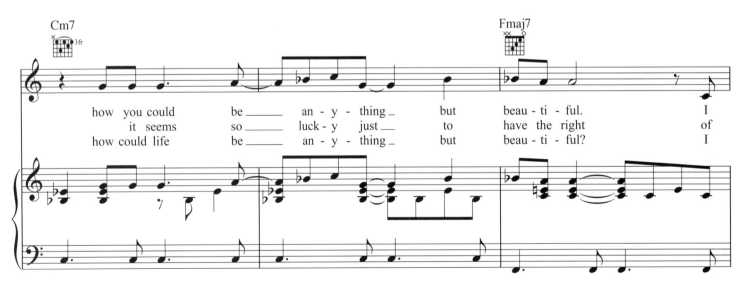

how you could   be _____ an - y - thing _ but   beau - ti - ful.   I
it seems   so _____ luck - y   just _____   to   have the right   of
how could life   be _____ an - y - thing _ but   beau - ti - ful?   I

Recorded a half step lower.

I'm tell - ing you _____ that you're

beau - ti - ful. _____

rit.

BITTER GREEN

Words and Music by
GORDON LIGHTFOOT

COTTON JENNY

Words and Music by
GORDON LIGHTFOOT

Moderately bright

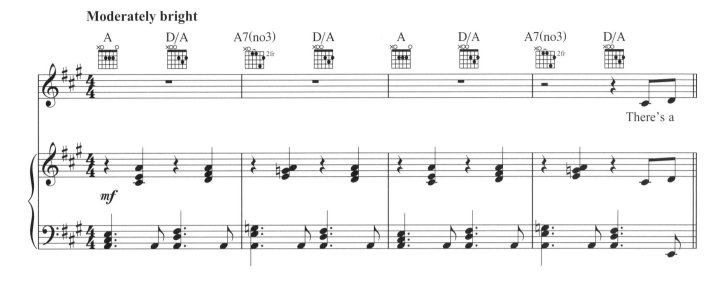

There's a

house _____ on a hill _____ by a worn-down, weath-ered old mill in the val-ley be-
new _____ day be-gins, _____ I go down to the cot - ton gin, and I make my
hot, _____ sick-ly South, _____ when they say, "Well, shut __ ma mouth," I can nev-er be

low where the riv-er winds; there's no such thing as bad times. And a
time worth - while to them, then I climb back up __ a - gain. And she
free from the cot-ton grind, but I know I got __ what's mine. A __

CANADIAN RAILROAD TRILOGY

Words and Music by
GORDON LIGHTFOOT

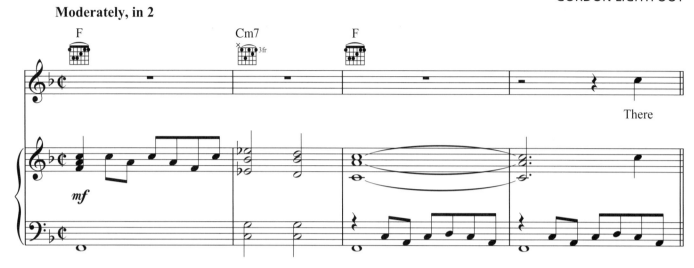

There

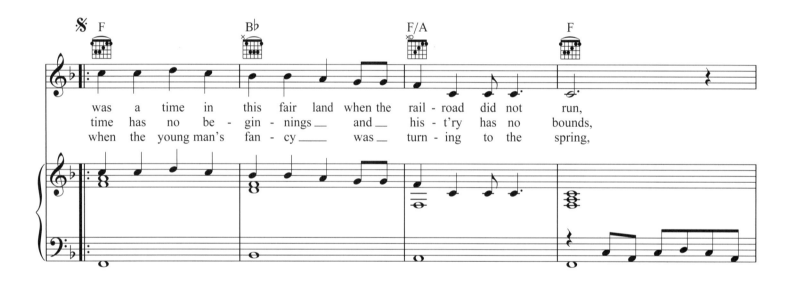

was a time in this fair land when the rail-road did not run,
time has no be - gin - nings __ and __ his-t'ry has no bounds,
when the young man's fan - cy __ was __ turn - ing to the spring,

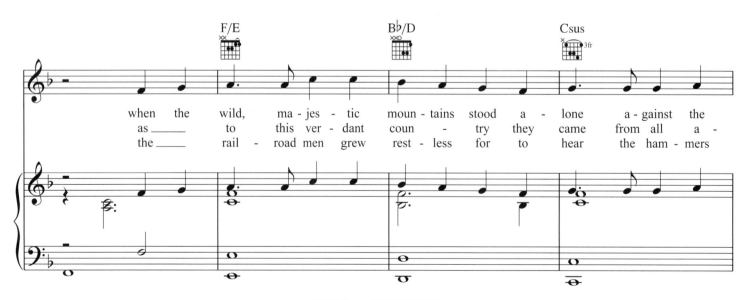

when the wild, ma - jes - tic moun - tains stood a - lone a - gainst the
as __ to this ver - dant coun - try they came from all a -
the __ rail - road men grew rest - less for to hear the ham - mers

CAREFREE HIGHWAY

Words and Music by
GORDON LIGHTFOOT

Pick-in' up the piec-es of my sweet, shat-tered dream, I
Turn-in' back the pag-es to the sweet times I love best, I
Search-in' through the frag-ments of my dream - shat-tered sleep, I

won-der how the old folks are to-night.
won-der if she'll ev-er do the same.
won-der if the years have closed her mind.

Her
Now the
Well, I

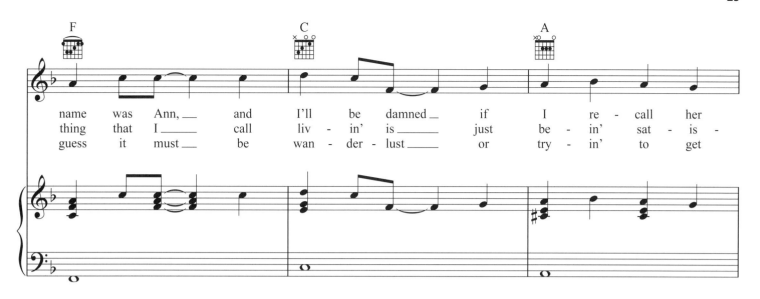

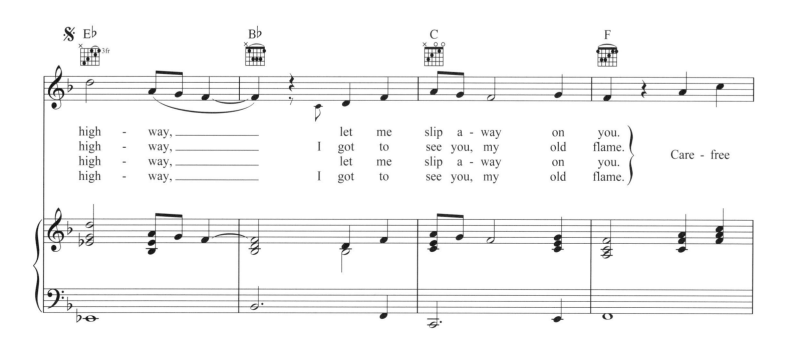

EARLY MORNIN' RAIN

Words and Music by
GORDON LIGHTFOOT

In the ear-ly morn - in' rain,
Out on run-way num - ber nine,
Hear the might-y en - gines roar,
This old air-port's got ___ me down.

with a dol - lar in ___ my hand,
big sev - en - oh - sev - en's set to go.
see the sil - ver wing ___ on high.
It's no earth - ly good ___ to me,

(That's What You Get)
FOR LOVIN' ME

Words and Music by
GORDON LIGHTFOOT

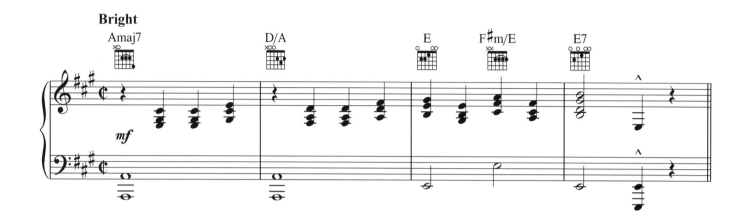

1. That's what you get for lov-in' me. ___
2.–5. *(See additional lyrics)*

That's what you get for lov-in' me. ___

Additional Lyrics

2. I ain't the kind to hang around
   With any new love that I found,
   'Cause movin' is my stock in trade.
   I'm movin' on,
   I won't think of you when I'm gone.

3. So don't you shed a tear for me,
   I ain't the love you thought I'd be.
   I got a hundred more like you.
   So don't be blue,
   I'll have a thousand 'fore I'm through.

4. Now, there you go, you're cryin' again.
   Now, there you go, you're cryin' again.
   But then, some day, when your poor heart
   Is on the mend,
   Well, I just might pass this way again.

5. That's what you get for lovin' me.
   That's what you get for lovin' me.
   Well, ev'rything you had is gone.
   As you can see,
   That's what you get for lovin' me.

I'M NOT SAYIN'

Words and Music by
GORDON LIGHTFOOT

I'm not say - in' that I love you.
I can't give my heart to you

I'm not say - in' that I'll care
or tell you that I'll sing your name

if you love
up to the

me.
sky.

I'm not say - in' that I'll care, I'm not
I can't lay the prom - ise down that I'll

IF YOU COULD READ MY MIND

Words and Music by
GORDON LIGHTFOOT

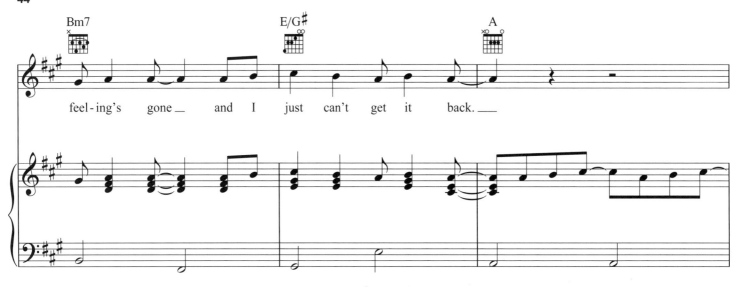

feel-ing's gone ___ and I just can't get it back. ___

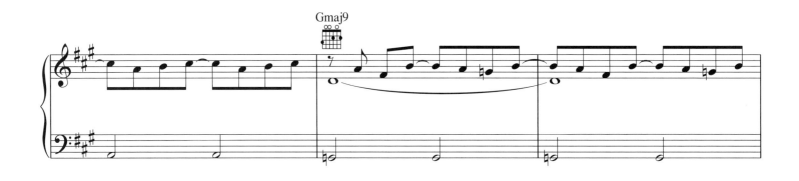

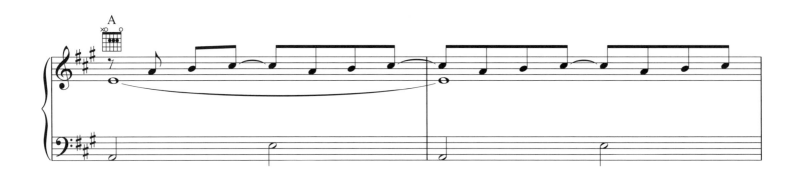

poco rit.

RAINY DAY PEOPLE

Words and Music by
GORDON LIGHTFOOT

Rain - y day peo - ple al - ways seem to know when it's time to call. __
If you get lone - ly, all you real - ly need is that rain - y day love. __
Instrumental
Rain - y day peo - ple al - ways seem to know when you're feel - in' blue. __

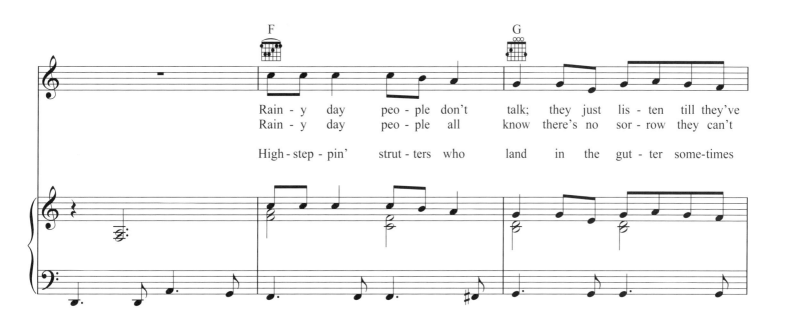

Rain - y day peo - ple don't talk; they just lis - ten till they've
Rain - y day peo - ple all know there's no sor - row they can't

High - step - pin' strut - ters who land in the gut - ter some - times

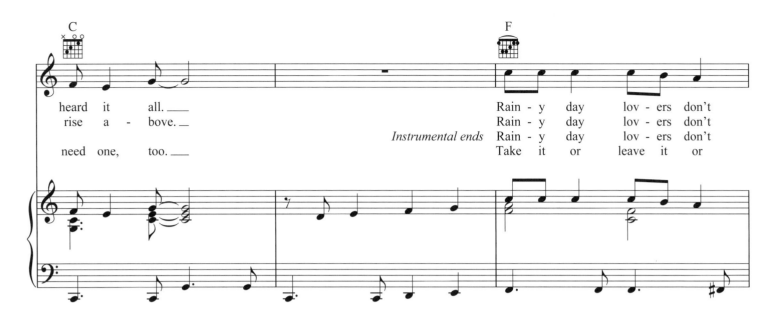

heard it all. ___
rise a - bove. ___
Instrumental ends Rain - y day lov - ers don't
need one, too. ___

Rain - y day lov - ers don't
Rain - y day lov - ers don't
Rain - y day lov - ers don't
Take it or leave it or

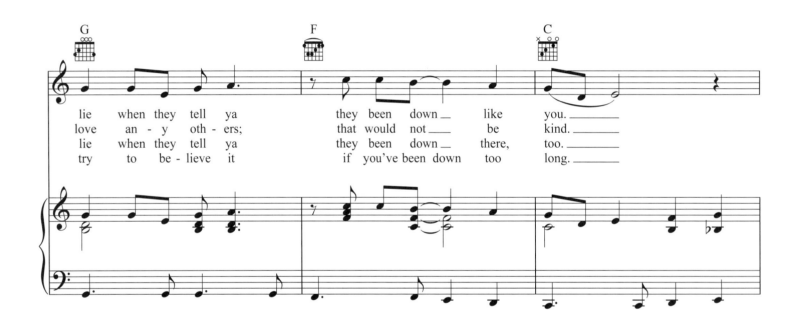

lie when they tell ya they been down ___ like you. _____
love an - y oth - ers; that would not ___ be kind. _____
lie when they tell ya they been down ___ there, too. _____
try to be - lieve it if you've been down too long. _____

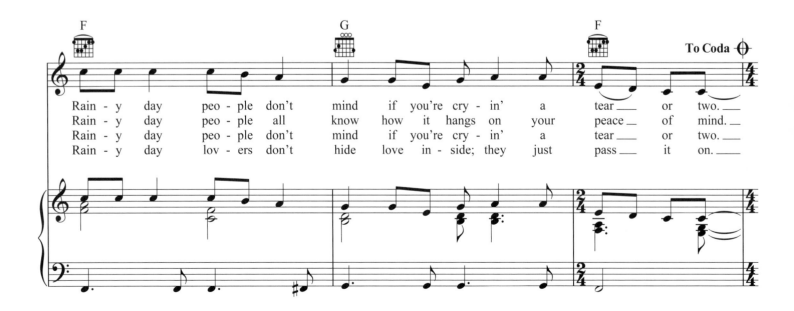

To Coda ⊕

Rain - y day peo - ple don't mind if you're cry - in' a tear ___ or two. ___
Rain - y day peo - ple all know how it hangs on your peace ___ of mind. ___
Rain - y day peo - ple don't mind if you're cry - in' a tear ___ or two. ___
Rain - y day lov - ers don't hide love in - side; they just pass ___ it on. ___

RIBBON OF DARKNESS

Words and Music by
GORDON LIGHTFOOT

SONG FOR A WINTER'S NIGHT

Words and Music by
GORDON LIGHTFOOT

Moderately, in 2

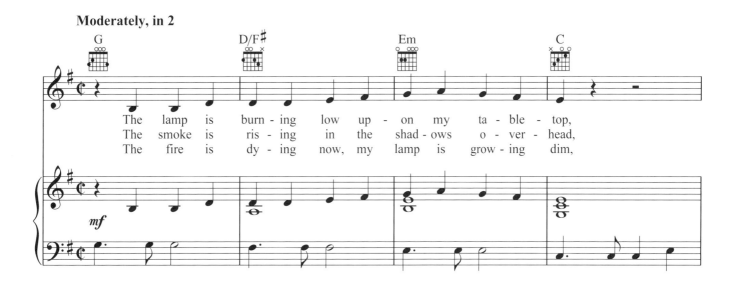

The lamp is burn - ing low up - on my ta - ble - top,
The smoke is ris - ing in the shad - ows o - ver - head,
The fire is dy - ing now, my lamp is grow - ing dim,

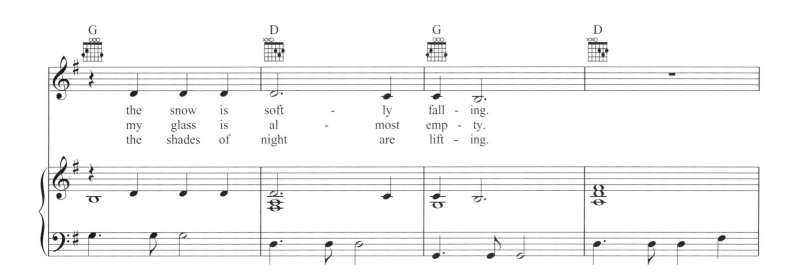

the snow is soft - ly fall - ing.
my glass is al - most emp - ty.
the shades of night are lift - ing.

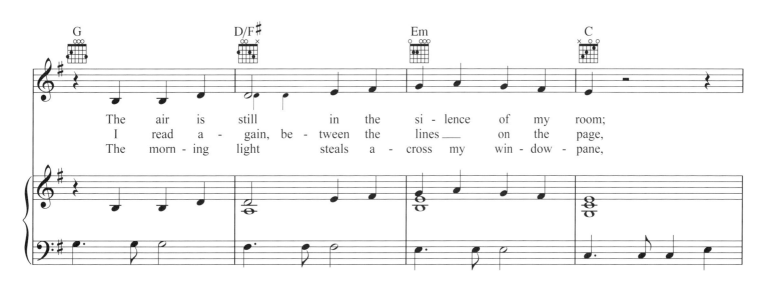

The air is still in the si - lence of my room;
I read a - gain, be - tween the lines ___ on the page,
The morn - ing light steals a - cross my win - dow - pane,

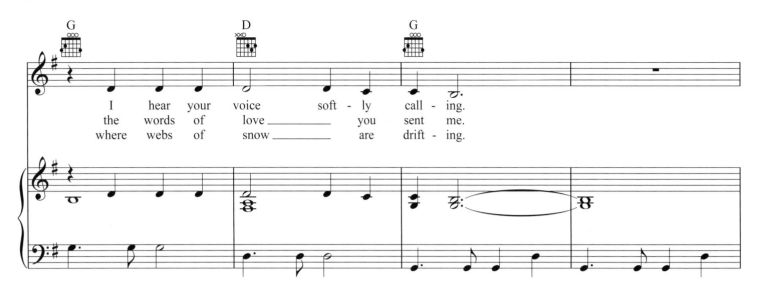

I hear your voice soft - ly call - ing.
the words of love _____ you sent me.
where webs of snow _____ are drift - ing.

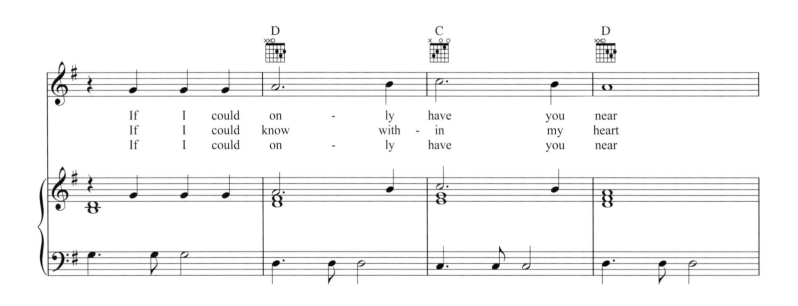

If I could on - ly have you near
If I could know with - in my heart
If I could on - ly have you near

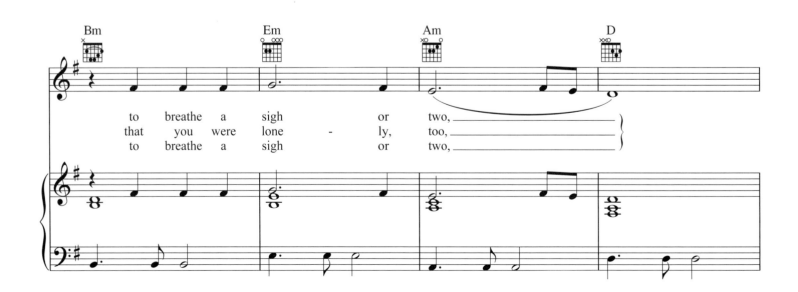

to breathe a sigh or two, _____
that you were lone - ly, too, _____
to breathe a sigh or two, _____

STEEL RAIL BLUES

Words and Music by
GORDON LIGHTFOOT

Moderately, in 2

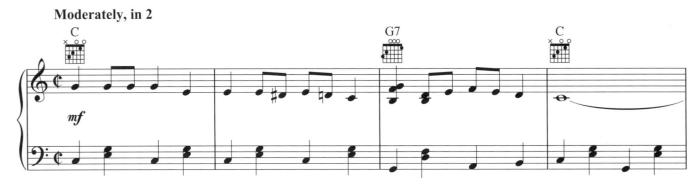

1. Well, I got my mail ___ late last night, a
2. been out here ___ man - y long days, I
3. been up - tight ___ most ev - 'ry night,

4., 5. *(See additional lyrics)*

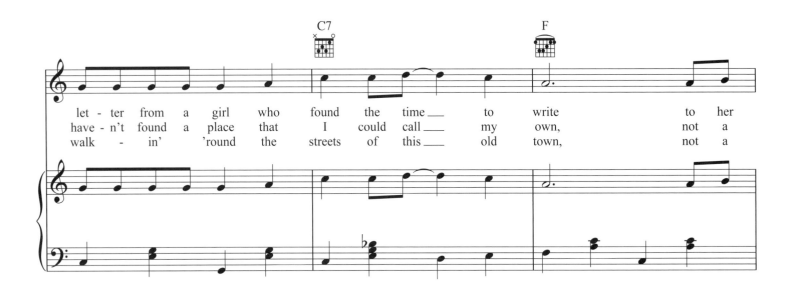

let - ter from a girl who found the time ___ to write to her
have - n't found a place that I could call ___ my own, not a
walk - in' 'round the streets of this ___ old town, not a

Ooh.

Additional Lyrics

4. Well, look over yonder across the plain:
   The big drive wheels a-poundin' along the ground.
   Gonna get on board and I'll be homeward bound.
   Now, I ain't had a home-cooked meal, and, Lord, I need one now.
   And the big steel rail gonna carry me home to the one I love.

5. Now, here I am with my hat in my hand,
   Standin' on the broad highway. Will you give a ride
   To a lonesome boy who missed the train last night?
   I went in town for one last round and I gambled my ticket away.
   And the big steel rail won't carry me home to the one I love.

SUNDOWN

Words and Music by
GORDON LIGHTFOOT

Recorded a half step lower.

first __ mis - take. ___ Sun - down, you bet - ter take care __ if I

find you been creep - in' 'round __ my back stairs. __ Some - times I

think it's a sin __ when I feel like I'm win - nin' when I'm los - in' a - gain. __

Play 6 times

Guitar solo ad lib.

TALKING IN YOUR SLEEP

Words and Music by
GORDON LIGHTFOOT

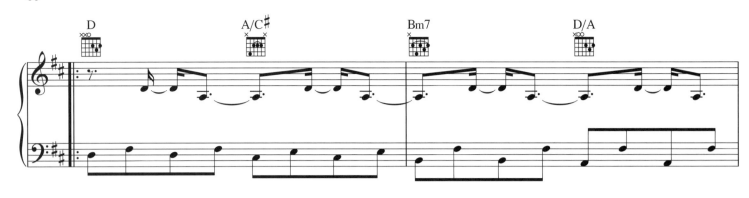

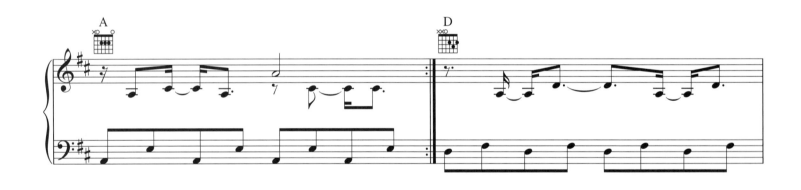

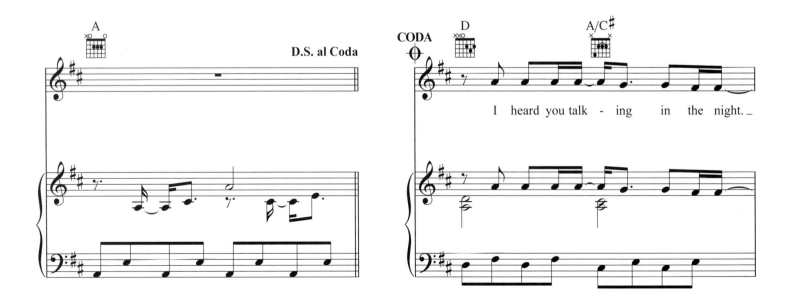

I heard you talk - ing in the night. _

THE WRECK OF THE EDMUND FITZGERALD

Words and Music by
GORDON LIGHTFOOT

Moderately slow, in 1

leg - end lives on from the Chip-pe-wa on down of the big lake they called "Git - che

2.–28. *(See additional lyrics)*

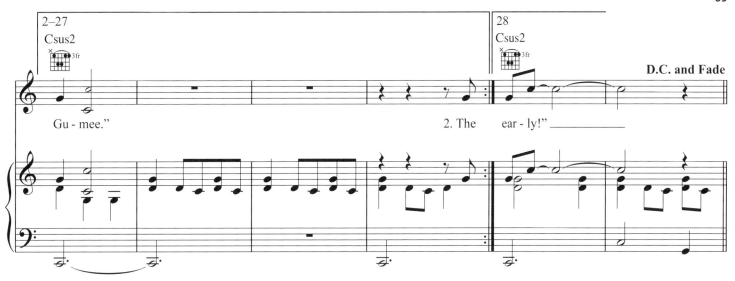

Additional Lyrics

2. The lake, it is said, never gives up her dead
   When the skies of November turn gloomy.

3. With a load of iron ore twenty-six thousand tons more
   Than the Edmund Fitzgerald weighed empty.

4. That good ship and true was a bone to be chewed
   When the gales of November came early.

5. The ship was the pride of the American side
   Coming back from some mill in Wisconsin.

6. As the big freighters go it was bigger than most
   With a crew and a captain well seasoned.

7. Concluding some terms with a couple of steel firms
   When they left fully loaded for Cleveland.

8. And later that night when the ship's bell rang,
   Could it be the north wind they'd been feelin'?

9. The wind in the wires made a tattletale sound
   And a wave broke over the railing.

10. And ev'ry man knew as the captain did too
    'Twas the witch of November come stealin'.

11. The dawn came late and the breakfast had to wait
    When the gales of November came slashin'.

12. When afternoon came it was freezin' rain
    In the face of a hurricane west wind.

13. When suppertime came the old cook came on deck
    Sayin', "Fellas, it's too rough t'feed ya."

14. At seven P.M. a main hatchway caved in;
    He said, "Fellas, it's been good t'know ya!"

15. The captain wired in he had water comin' in
    And the good ship and crew was in peril.

16. And later that night when 'is lights went outta sight
    Came the wreck of the Edmund Fitzgerald.

17. Does anyone know where the love of God goes
    When the waves turn the minutes to hours?

18. The searchers all say they'd have made Whitefish Bay
    If they'd put fifteen more miles behind 'er.

19. They might have split up or they might have capsized;
    They might have broke deep and took water.

20. And all that remains is the faces and the names
    Of the wives and the sons and the daughters.

21. Lake Huron rolls, Superior sings
    In the rooms of her ice-water mansion.

22. Old Michigan steams like a young man's dreams;
    The islands and bays are for sportsmen,

23. And farther below Lake Ontario
    Takes in what Lake Erie can send her.

24. And the iron boats go as the mariners all know
    With the Gales of November remembered.

25. In a musty old hall in Detroit they prayed,
    In the "Maritime Sailors' Cathedral."

26. The church bell chimed 'til it rang twenty-nine times
    For each man on the Edmund Fitzgerald,

27. The legend lives on from the Chippewa on down
    Of the big lake they called "Gitche Gumee."

28. "Superior," they said, "never gives up her dead
    When the gales of November come early!"

SUMMER SIDE OF LIFE

Words and Music by
GORDON LIGHTFOOT

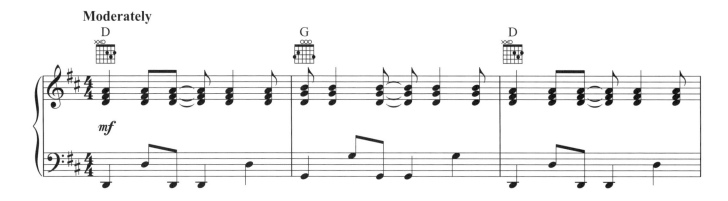

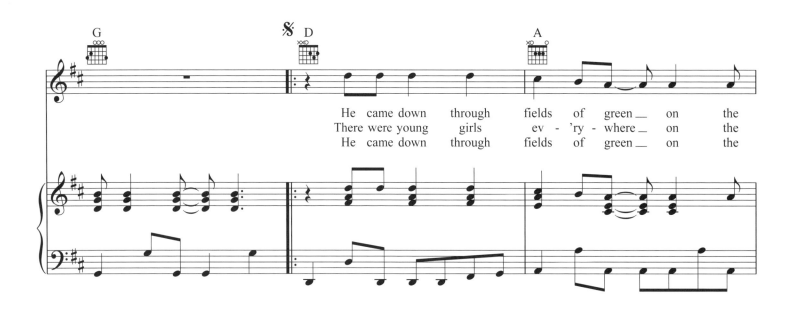

He came down through fields of green ___ on the
There were young girls ev - 'ry - where ___ on the
He came down through fields of green ___ on the

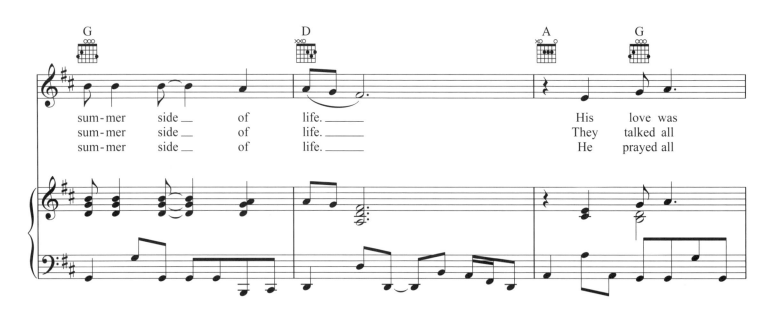

sum - mer side ___ of life. _____ His love was
sum - mer side ___ of life. _____ They talked all
sum - mer side ___ of life. _____ He prayed all